Queen Charlotte

CHERRY LAKE PRESS

Published in the United States of America by Cherry Lake Publishing Group
Ann Arbor, Michigan
www.cherrylakepublishing.com

Reading Adviser: Beth Walker Gambro, MS, Ed., Reading Consultant, Yorkville, IL
Book Design: Jennifer Wahi
Illustrator: Jeff Bane

Photo Credits: © Stefan Braeutigam/Shutterstock, 5; © P Maxwell Photography/Shutterstock, 7; Sir Joshua Reynolds, Public domain, via Wikimedia Commons, 9 and 22; Johan Zoffany, Public domain, via Wikimedia Commons, 11; National Trust, Public domain, via Wikimedia Commons, 13; © Magdalena Kucova, 15 and 23; Thomas Rowlandson (1756–1827) and Augustus Charles Pugin (1762–1832) (after) John Bluck (fl. 1791–1819), Joseph Constantine Stadler (fl. 1780–1812), Thomas Sutherland (1785–1838), J. Hill, and Harraden (aquatint engravers)[1], Public domain, via Wikimedia Commons, 17; © After Nathaniel Whittock, CC BY 4.0 via Wikimedia Commons, 19; Benjamin West, Public domain, via Wikimedia Commons, 21

Cherry Lake Press is an imprint of Cherry Lake Publishing Group

Library of Congress Cataloging-in-Publication Data

Names: Loh-Hagan, Virginia, author. | Bane, Jeff, 1957- illustrator.
Title: Queen Charlotte / written by: Virginia Loh-Hagan ; illustrator: Jeff Bane
Description: Ann Arbor : Cherry Lake Publishing, [2024] | Series: My itty-bitty bio | Audience: Grades K-1 | Summary: "Queen Charlotte was Queen of Great Britain and Ireland and may have been Britain's first Black queen. This biography for early readers examines her life in a simple, age-appropriate way that helps young readers develop word recognition and reading skills. This title helps all readers learn about a historical female leader who made a difference in our world. The My Itty-Bitty Bio series celebrates diversity and inclusion, values that readers of all ages can aspire to"-- Provided by publisher.
Identifiers: LCCN 2023035031 | ISBN 9781668937778 (hardcover) | ISBN 9781668938812 (paperback) | ISBN 9781668940150 (ebook) | ISBN 9781668941508 (pdf)
Subjects: LCSH: Charlotte, Queen, consort of George III, King of Great Britain, 1744-1818--Juvenile literature. | Queens--Great Britain--Biography--Juvenile literature. | Great Britain--History--George III, 1760-1820--Juvenile literature.
Classification: LCC DA506.A3 L64 2023 | DDC 941.07/3092--dc23/eng/20230809
LC record available at https://lccn.loc.gov/2023035031

Printed in the United States of America
Corporate Graphics

About the author: When not writing, Dr. Virginia Loh-Hagan serves as the Director of the Asian Pacific Islander Desi American (APIDA) Center at San Diego State University. She is also the Co-Executive Director of The Asian American Education Project. She lives in San Diego with her very tall husband and very naughty dogs.

About the illustrator: Jeff Bane and his two business partners own a studio along the American River in Folsom, California, home of the 1849 Gold Rush. When Jeff's not sketching or illustrating for clients, he's either swimming or kayaking in the river to relax.

I was born in 1744. I was German.
I lived in a small area.

I was **noble**. My family were rulers.
I was a princess.

George III was king. He ruled England. I married him. I moved there.

Have you ever moved
to a new place?

George III got sick. I was loyal to him. We had 15 children. Our children became leaders.

I was different. Some think I had Black family members. I may be England's first Black queen.

I loved art. I loved music. I loved plants. I decorated Christmas trees.

Do you like music?

I was popular. Places are named for me. A plant was named for me.

I **founded** hospitals. I helped **orphans**. I founded homes for them.

19

I died in 1818. But my **legacy** lives on. I ruled for 57 years.

What would you like to ask me?

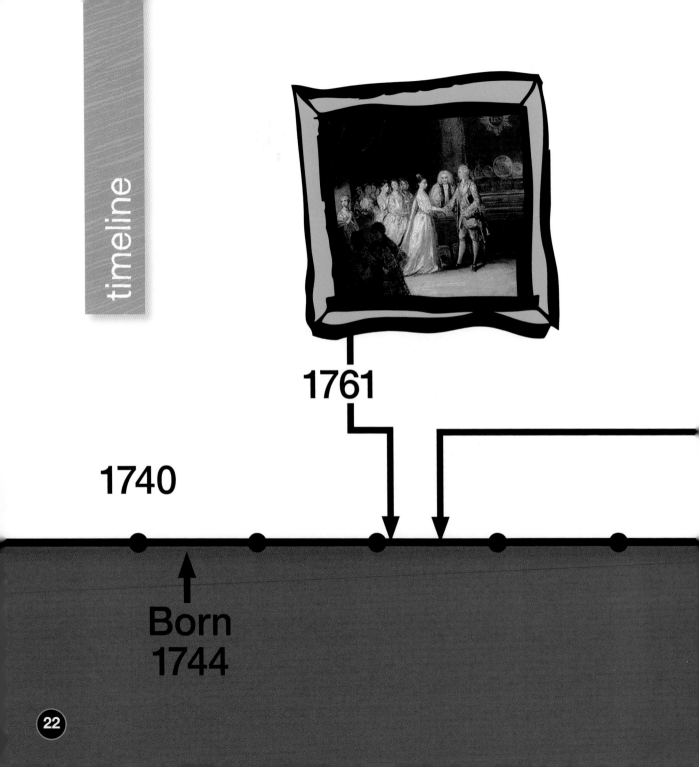

1761

1740

Born
1744

1764

1840

↑
Died
1818

23

glossary

founded (FOWND-ed) to start a project to build something new

legacy (LEH-guh-see) anything passed down from a person in the past

noble (NOH-buhl) having royal blood

orphans (OR-fuhns) children without parents

index